# How Bills Become Laws

## Children's Modern History

**BABY PROFESSOR**

EDUCATION KIDS

Speedy Publishing LLC
40 E. Main St. #1156
Newark, DE 19711
www.speedypublishing.com
Copyright 2016

Laws keep a society's order and
help it function in a fair
and orderly manner.

In the absence of laws, society will lose its purpose and discipline, and this may jeopardize all the progress it has made culturally, morally, and technologically. Moreover, criminal activity rises when there are no good laws, or the laws cannot be enforced.

How a Bill starts.
In the United States
of America, as well
as other parts of
the world, a law
begins as an idea.

The Bill is proposed. That idea will become a bill when one person working in the congress tells another congressperson about it. This will lead to the sponsorship of that idea by a group of members of congress.

Introduction of the Bill. The bill is promoted by its sponsors in the Congress and also in public. After the introduction of the bill, it will make its way to the Committee assigned to handle the specific concerns covered by it. For example, if the bill is related to animal husbandry, then it will be passed to the Agriculture Committee.

Committee Action. The committee studies and debates the bill, and "mark it up". "Marking up" is proposing changes to the text.

To determine whether it should be approved or rejected, the committee takes a vote on the bill. If the bill gets approval from the committee, it is forwarded to either the House of Representatives or the Senate.

Consideration on House Floor. To permit faster consideration, most bills are debated, a practice known as the Committee of the Whole. This lets the Senate or the House set aside many rules of procedure while discussing the bill. Special rules could also be granted specifically for the bill under consideration.

After the debate, the bill is read a second time. This reading is a section-by-section approach, and amendments may be suggested. After this is done, there is a third reading of the bill as amended, and then finally, the House or the Senate is ready to vote on the bill.

The Bill is put to Vote. The Bill is read by its title only when the bill is ready to be voted on. Members will vote to pass the bill by a Yea or Nay vote. They could also choose not to vote even though they are present. In this case they will just declare themselves as 'present.' Members cast their vote electronically using the Electronic Voting System.

If a majority of the House voted to pass the bill, it is then passed on to the Senate for a similar process. For a bill originating in the Senate, if it passes there, then it is sent to the House for a concurring vote.

The Bill is referred to the Senate or House. Once a bill has been passed on to the other house for review, it is said to be 'engrossed.' The bill may be sent to a specific committee for study or markup. Members may choose to ignore the bill, vote against the bill, or vote in favor of the bill.

If a bill passes one house, and then passes in the second house with slightly different language, it has to be sent for further review by a conference committee made up of members from both the House and Senate. Any differences in the languages of the House and the Senate versions must be resolved before the bill will be sent to the President.

Bill Sent To President. The President has three choices when a bill reaches him. He can:

Sign the bill—which means that the bill becomes a law.

Veto or refuse to sign the bill—this will bring the bill back to the House and the Senate, with the reasons for the veto. The two houses can then try to hold a vote to override the veto.

Each house must vote to override by a two-thirds majority; if both do, then the bill becomes law. Otherwise, the bill is vetoed and does not become law.

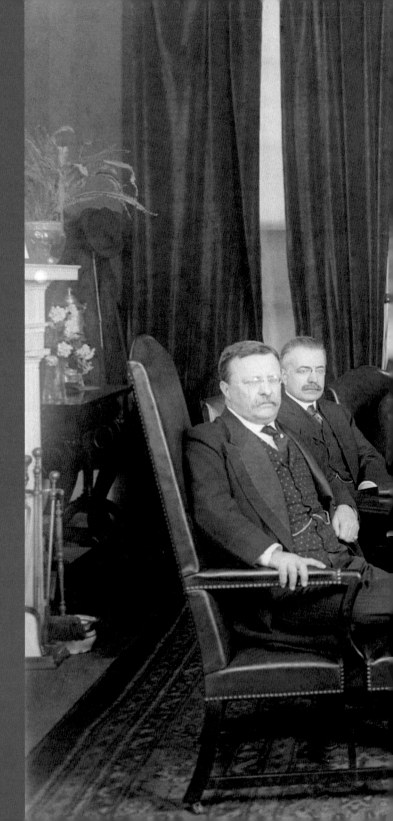

Pocket veto or do nothing— after 10 days if Congress is in session, the bill automatically becomes a law. However, if the Congress is not in session, the bill does not become a law.

These are the steps that are needed to make a Bill become a Law in the United States government.

Visit

**BABY PROFESSOR**
EDUCATION KIDS

# www.BabyProfessorBooks.com

to download Free Baby Professor eBooks and view
our catalog of new and exciting Children's Books

Made in the USA
Monee, IL
17 April 2022